To David
R.A.

To Mabel Hammond Bulmirri Beverstock –
a beautiful creature, whom I've never yet met!
L.M.

ORCHARD BOOKS
338 Euston Road, London NW1 3BH

Orchard Books Australia
Level 17/207, Kent Street, Sydney, NSW 2000

First published by Orchard Books in 2009

Text copyright © Ronda Armitage 2009
Illustrations copyright © Layn Marlow 2009

The rights of Ronda Armitage to be identified as the author
and of Layn Marlow to be identified as the illustrator
of this work have been asserted by them in accordance
with the Copyright, Designs and Patents Act, 1988.

A CIP catalogue record for this book
is available from the British Library.

ISBN 978 1 40830 186 9
1 3 5 7 9 10 8 6 4 2

Printed in China

Orchard Books is a division of Hachette Children's Books,
an Hachette UK company.

www.hachette.co.uk

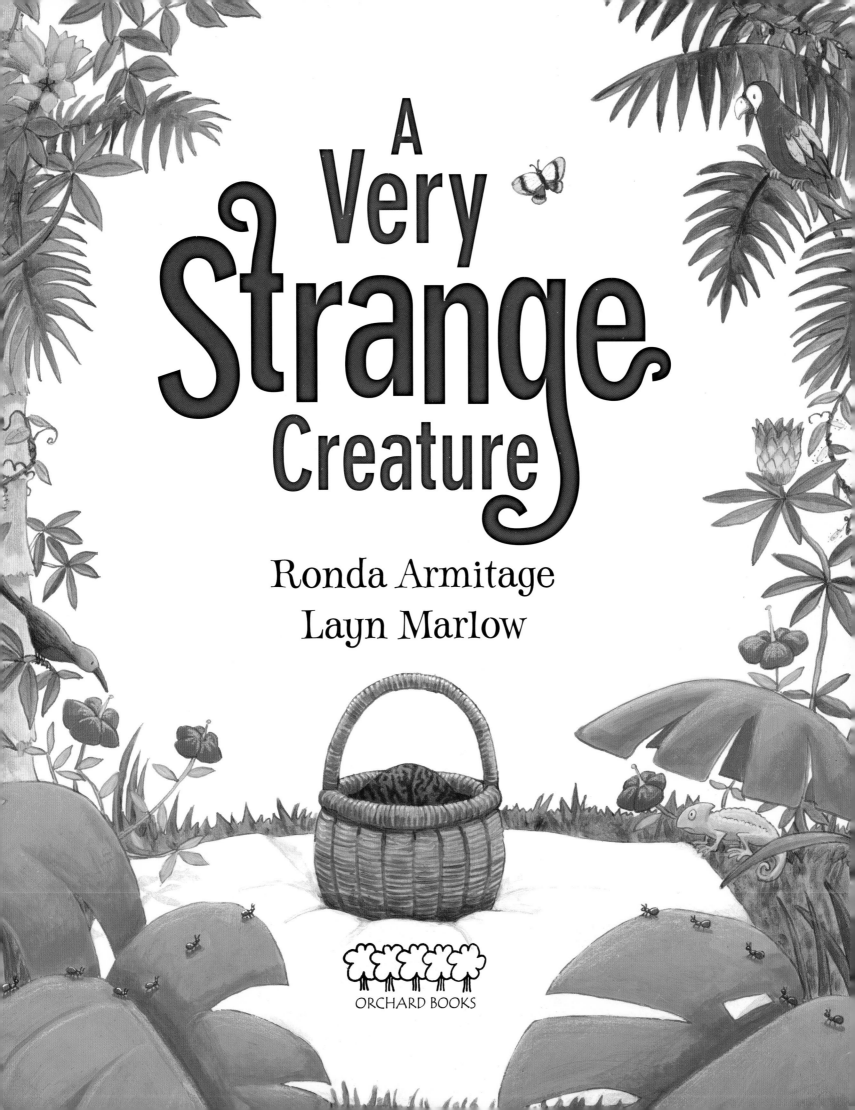

A Very Strange Creature

Ronda Armitage

Layn Marlow

ORCHARD BOOKS

At the edge of the jungle

something

stirred . . .

Monkey saw it first.
He stopped playing
and peered down.

"What a
strange creature!"
he said.
"Whatever can it be?"

And he swung off
through the trees.

Elephant was
having a bath.

"Elephant, Elephant!"
cried Monkey.
"I've found a
strange creature.
Follow me!"

"Whatever can it be?"
asked Elephant.
"It hasn't got a trunk.
How does it wash
without a trunk?
It'll get very smelly."

Giraffe was
finishing
her lunch.

"And it hasn't got a tail,"
chattered Monkey.
"How can it swing
without a tail?
Giraffe might know
what it is."

"I'll come immediately," she said.

Giraffe tipped her head
to see the strange creature.
"M-m-m-m," she murmured.
"It has a very short neck.
How will it reach the trees?
Poor little creature,
how hungry it must be."

Frog hopped up.
"Well I never. Whatever
can it be?" he croaked.

"It is a
strange creature.
No trunk, no tail,
    and a very short neck.

And just look at
those feet!
How can it swim
with feet like that?"

"Lion will know
what it is," said Giraffe.

"Let's ask him."

Lion growled.
"Go away! I'm trying to sleep."

"Oh please, Great Lion," whispered Monkey.
"Come and see.
There's a strange creature."

"What a funny little thing," Lion purred. "It hasn't any fur. How can it keep warm if it hasn't any fur?

No trunk for washing.

No tail for swinging.

No neck for reaching high.

No webbed feet for swimming.

No fur for keeping warm . . .

It is a
very strange creature."

Lion puffed out his chest.

"I'm an extremely
brave lion.
I'll ask it what it is."

Lion cleared his throat.
"Excuse me, Very Strange Creature,
but I'm asking most politely . . .

Please could you tell me what you are?"

The **very strange creature**
gazed up at Lion,
opened its mouth,
and said . . .

"Waa-aa

"Thank you," purred Lion.
He turned to the other animals.

"This
very strange creature
is called a
waa-aa-aa."

"A
waa-aa-aa?"
croaked Frog.
"But what can a
waa-aa-aa
do?"

Someone came running.
"Hush, my baby, hush.
It's just the animals
come to see."

"A baby?" said Monkey.

"This
very strange creature
is not a waa-aa-aa,
it's a baby?
But what can a baby do?"

"This baby
makes me happy,"
said the mother.
"This baby makes me
dance and sing.

This baby smiles at everyone.
Smile,
Baby,
smile."

"Ahhhh," said all the animals.
"So that's what it can do.
Thank you, happy baby."

And the animals
smiled too ...